you teach me light

you teach me light

slightly dangerous poems

Melaney Poli

Foreword by Jeanie Tomasko

RESOURCE *Publications* · Eugene, Oregon

YOU TEACH ME LIGHT
slightly dangerous poems

Resource Publications
An Imprint of Wipf and Stock Publishers
199 W. 8th Ave., Suite 3
Eugene, OR 97401

www.wipfandstock.com

PAPERBACK ISBN: 978-1-5326-4772-7
HARDCOVER ISBN: 978-1-5326-4773-4
EBOOK ISBN: 978-1-5326-4774-1

Manufactured in the U.S.A.   05/01/18

To the memory of Shelly L Hall
1958-2010 poet of search

Marianne Dora Rein
1911-1941 poet of hope
and of

David S Flom
1948-2015 some teacher

Sie lehren mich Licht

The whole of life lives in the verb "seeing."

—Pierre Teilhard de Chardin

Contents

Foreword

It's like walking into an old shop filled with drawers; each drawer contains a map and each map wants to take you. The poems in *You teach me light* take you to a place you've been but didn't really see, a place you've not been but ache to see, a place that will teach you light, yes, and that "art . . . demands total faith, even surrender, maybe the death of the life you walked in with." Poli's small maps take you everywhere you must go if you want to walk out of the shop and "days and months later know you have not breathed the same way since."

Jeanie Tomasko

Acknowledgements

Anglican Theological Review: Arizona; variation and fugue on a happy liturgical typo; You teach me light

The Christian Century: Salzburg, Republic of Austria, July 2006; Horizons

Clare: Ursa Vestiarii

Julian's Window: from a manual on forgiveness

RightHandPointing: Thank you for small beginnings

Thank you for small beginnings

for the edge of the sheet tucked back
the pillowcase pulled on, thank you
for the one corner swept, the linen
basket filled, for one box emptied,
one letter begun, for one spoon washed,
one verse of a poem written down,

for one shoe placed
neatly by another, the needle threaded,
the first page read, thank you, thank you,
thank you

the monk who wrote himself to death

In this world one collects things, you see,
and to some certain falls the thankless chore

of garnering words, stringing them one
upon another, and if you're auspicious,

relinquishing them at a profit (it's known
as selling one's soul). To be sure,

for the prophets the cost will be higher,
the collection more probing and pitiless;

and depending on the lie of your fears
your words are a net, or a fire:

a snare your readers can catch you in, or your hell
of feeding an insatiable blaze.

And either way it's a hall of mirrors,
where each beaded word tricks the light,

and no amount of spooling will spell
any certain escape from this maze.

There is a way out of course, and quite
simple: the ring of fire, the breath

of air, and the land beyond guile
and names. You can get there by prayer—

or by letting go of knowing the way,
both are the same: a kind of death

to what was before, with a smile
that knows there is nothing to say.

On missing my tour of the St John's Bible, Collegeville, Minnesota

Of course it sucks. I didn't come a thousand miles and bucks
to get disappointed this much. I expected crême brulée, got
a mouthful of baking powder. Scrubbed out my expectations.
Some mistake.

I like to think art has an answer to everything; it's an artist's sin.
Maybe I just wanted to get smashed on beauty, stoned on lovely
adjectives. Or maybe the hope that beholding will make me
able to see.

Should I say (I who have learned, something) God you are my
best illumination, it's by your being that I see? Should I rather say
I now go out and see people like illuminations, walking? Perhaps
I don't know my power

or perhaps I don't desire. And I know nothing would ever be
enough, and yet I will go on craving. I have an artist's most
irrational faith in what can be made from what seems to be
nothing. See,

I could say *Was mich nicht umbringt, macht mich stärker*, or
that it brings me to my senses, or strips me of illusion, or
that there is every possibility that what I don't see can still
illuminate me.

Fable

Let me touch one soul by my art, he said. I have a fire.
But he wondered: what if the whole world refuses to hear?

He was good for a while at throwing brilliant bouquets
of words. He could make you see with a splash of vowels.
Color your mind by metaphors, story. Editors loved
him. What happened? If you're reading this,

he found the real diamond, better bliss,
an end large enough to surpass all he loved.
He revised to the woods, stopped publishing. The owls
survey his notebooks, words for the sky, not bookcases.

There are unknown splendors in every corner, without fear.
He will have a bonfire some night, without regret, or desire.

Arizona

On a small island
in the green water of a harbor
a ship sits upright on the sandy bottom
barely visible in clouds of murk and hearsay
under my eight- nine- ten-year old feet.
Beautiful Hawai'i has on her endless summer.
On a day like this things were blown to pieces.
"Men died here": but it doesn't translate
to my experience. The circle of island
sits in a sky of perfect light. Only the sun
breaks on these waves. The ship is berthed
in its own past, its sky too remote to imagine.

It's the first place I remember, tall blue
over adobe wall, the roadrunner highlighted
like a flash of lightning. The light was like
another world, white shouting, forever
in my eye. Everything was gathered,
every measure fled. Everywhere,
to this day, the sky is Arizona.

The Jewish Bride

for Ruth Valerio

She ran away with another man, he said.
He took to gardening every weekend,
his allotment a little island of sanity

at the edge of Berlin. He rebuffed
well-meaning friends, wanted to tend
his cabbages undisturbed. Each week

he took a basket and a different book
to picnic in the Rosenkohl. After a few years
there were only potatoes to till, but it was still

his oasis from the terror of war or grief,
a place to bring the solace of black market
Lachs, French wine, the baker's last loaf,

fifty square meters he could call the future.
Around him the world spun out of control.
He used Mark notes to stuff the cracks in the shed,

brought blankets and rags, mementoes, a rug.
When the Allies came, he opened the door
and led her, thin and pale and well read,

in the circle of his arms in the sunlight.
Every night was Passover, she said.

Big Clouds Far Away

the wind blew hard all night
I tossed, threw off blankets, didn't dream
woke to the sound of thunder, worried
had I left something out

at dawn there was a shorn sky, white
hazed, and big clouds far away

I mowed the lawn slowly, thinking
of tornadoes, disease, love
all the things that could roar over unannounced
anything that could sweep me away

Salzburg, Republic of Austria, July 2006

In order not to repeat history, it is not enough to know it,
we must know ourselves, and our complicity.

    —Schilling

Some days you have to take what you can get
and that day my mother was too sick
to find yet one more crowded pavement café

and the worst of it was, sitting there in
my habit, I had to see it all unfold: the tired
couple with their small child, the empty table

and the promise of refreshment, and then
the waiter descending in a blaze of jeers,
scathing looks and torrid gestures, and watch

the husband and wife gather their dignity
and leave, unwelcome only for the offense
of resembling too much the enemy du jour

and I had nowhere to go to, nowhere to
hide my shame, no means of protest when
the waiter returned and served us sweetly,

set the coffee before me, and the only way
I could ask *is a veil any better than a chador?*
was to say, simply, *Dankeschön*

Belonging

Name a place: even the sounds
tell the tale. And gravity, distance, distort.
The stars over Germany in winter swung the whole sky
northward, past the clay tiles around my rooftop window
I could lean out and watch a cold dawn blot them into day

Hawai'i was nothing but sun or rain or vowels, all
a matter of light, cloud, dirt, wind, blue and green
We learned about places impossibly far away
Stars, when they came, spilled wider than the ocean

Somewhere they shone over other places
over you, over the Dutch flag that I was convinced
was that of every nation, even over the dark wake
of the midnight ferry from Oostende

the crooked finger of the Chesapeake
that surprised me from the plane. Home must be
where I tend to, the tongue I am understood. Its weight
changes the shape of everything, each tale telling
every sound, every place in one name.

process of conversion

1 impasse
they wanted me to conduct *Second Waltz*
for a high school orchestra class
and I thought one part went in 3/4
and one in 2/2
and the sign for the time
was the symbol for infinity
everything disorganized
and last minute and late
looking for parts, stands and chairs
I don't recall even beginning

2 epiphany
on a ship on an icy sea being "chased" by an ice floe
and you didn't know if it ended as a shipwreck or not
and I was thinking "I am so *tired* of shipwrecks!"

3 breakthrough
I was instrumental in saving the government of a small African nation from
overthrow by two women.

4 taking stock
Photographs, and
digging in a park in a depressed area of France
with a boy and girl, and we uncovered beautiful
mineral stones in labels, but who had thrown them away?

5 orientation
A rock musician, hugely popular
wore nothing but white
even his hair
"He was different from the others
because when we told him to die
he did, and was very happy."

6 perseverance

We kept running into members of Dave Matthews Band,
and someone told them about the book. One of them said
he wanted to see it sometime. I was flattered, I didn't think
he was serious. I was in my room reading when he suddenly
walked in and said "Well, where is it?" and I thought
"Oh gosh, he really wants to see it,
what have I been doing?"

Ursa Vestiarii

the bear got out of the closet
it had been rattling the doorknob
for several months but I ignored it

then one day it took the door
off the hinges, stormed out snarling
and mauled me in an unfriendly way

until, worn out by these exertions,
it fell asleep, dreaming of mauling

and there it lies, mountain of bear
sawing logs in the doorway,
impossible to push in
or shut the door on,

no goldilocks guest that could
listen to reason and be persuaded, you know,
there are better accommodations elsewhere,

nor any natural specimen
specializing in bugs and berries
who could docilely be tempted to
a more suitable habitat

but a species at home with me
indifferent to my preferences in the matter
fond of dark places and corners

whose fitful slumbering growls
break into my nights
and leave me awake and wondering

why we can't make better arrangements
and how long this can go on

Ursa Illectatii

I thought I had wised up, come to my senses,
finally arrived where I had the good sense

to turn away when I smelled it coming,
not to run over to it breathlessly, bare my veins,

not to wave my hopes in its face—to say,
"Screw you! I've got better stuff to do," yet

here I am again, putting out my choice cuts,
just *waiting* for what's-his-face to come along

and shred me to pulp. You'd think
you'd think, I had learned long ago, but somehow

I keep coming up with this absurd need
to taunt the bear: "You come here and take a bite

out of me if you dare!" I know very well it will,
as long as I want it to.

Ursa Supplicatrix

I don't work when the bear works.
The bear works effectively. I drop it all,
effect, affect, anything passing for courtesy.
I just do survival. Play at full volume

Appalachian cello, Chopin etudes,
wash with lavender soap, gorge
chocolate. Try to find the least painful
way to exist, the most painful way to live.

Once, skunk-drunk with agony
I staggered up to the bear as it slept
turned up its big paws and pronounced
very loudly (not caring if it woke):

"Now *look*, you will *pray*, like this.
It's not hard, just lie there, open
your paws, snore if you must.
Don't try too hard. *Relax*.

All you have to do is be still.
Get used to it. Pray a *lot*.
You should learn to pray
without ceasing."

Ursa Scaenae

Exit, pursued by a bear

    —Shakespeare, *A Winter's Tale*

                 But
the bear's a mere scrim. Why should it follow?
I was not born for this—to be hounded out
by a nothing, a bit of scenery.

When cued I shall go forth unencumbered
pursued by nothing but what goes before:
the hospitable love that kept me safe.

I am not gone forever; I am real.
The bear is lost without me, and no more.

Ursa Saltatrix

Bear be not proud, though some have found thee
toothed and terrible, for thou art not so.
For those, whom thou think'st thou dost overthrow
fall not, poor bear, nor yet canst thou fell me.
From worst despair, which but thy lackey be,
We are delivered—and from thee as well.
Thou art no master, nor eternal, though
For one brief hour thy tarantella thrall
The quiet mind, grip soul in agony.
Thou art a slave to grace, and medicine,
And though I writhe a space beneath thy spell
And weep and wail, yet still I shall be well
And better than before; why swell'st thou then?
The worst thou wield'st is but a passing trance,
Thou shalt be tamed, for good; bear, thou shalt dance.

How to get out of Rembrandt

Lost in Middleton once
I put my hand in the car door pocket
hoping for a map of Madison
but instead withdrew *A Guide
to Rembrandt*, left there after
a museum trip. I don't know
what this fat Dutch guy, broke,
can tell me about the way
from the airport to 94, but
maybe there's something he knows
about seeing light, and how
to follow it, about the paths
of color that inexorably steer
the eye, and something about
getting home by ways
other than lines, something
defiant, even tender, in the freedom
of this brushwork, that can get me
to hate driving a little less,
enough to let the road unfold
before me in a gratuitous tableaux
of discovery, enough to get me
to the Beltline breathing light,
less afraid of shadow, or loss.

location, location

After the reading a young woman wants to know
from where we get our ideas. She's earnest, willing

to learn. I'm lost for words. What can I say? from
stones in my pockets? or God? or my dark corners

and stairways? Should I say my metaphor meter
is set too high? It could all be mistakes—spilled

milk, Freudian slippages, good trips, childhood
rubble. Maybe my magnetic field. Maybe I have

a nose for them. Should I just admit they find me
like trouble? that once, they came gushing out

of a hose? got lodged in my sandal? Or confess
"Who cares? I'm in love with the shapes of sounds.

I get loaded on resonance"? One of the other poets
says "Nobody knows where poetry comes from."

She might be right. But I want to warn the young
woman: Save your barking—you won't tree a poem.

Where isn't a response. Let everything touch you.
Make way. It's unplugged, like love, it doesn't know

here or there.

enough

what you're really twisting around in, of course, are your limitations.
    —flannery o'connor

sketch
      the cap won't screw off
      burnt umber, Rembrandt blue
      madder lake. I'm left with
      indigo, ochre, titanium. "Such
      a restrained palette," the curator
      notes admiringly. "Such a refined
      sense of color, such discretion."

study
      our art teacher wouldn't let us
      use black. "See differently. Use
      other means to say what you mean."
      Later, I painted
      like Rouault in revenge
      to learn when to say when

final version
      for years I've been careful—
      Today I need to be wastrel
      chop boards, slop turpentine
      splurge an entire tube of indigo
      in the service of a line. Make
      a mess, see if more is less
      I'll split the tubes that won't open
      I can't live by lies and halves

What poetry wants

sometimes it aspires to be music, wants to be your dance
but what it really wants is to be prisms
wind-holes, kaleidoscopes

it wants to be the sulfur, the contact
between the match and the flame, wants
to be what salts, lights, frays your ordinary
the edge of the abyss, the pebble over the rim

wants to be the sound of one hand clapping
wants to be the world tilted on its side
wants to be the tiny piece of gravel shifting around in your shoe

the surprise of butterflies blowing around you
the scalpel that removes something hard from your soul

it wants to be what knocks the wind out of you
wants to be the wind that gets in your head, bones, dreams

the thin blade of want wedged in your ribs
that you don't know what it is

except that you know you read something,
somewhere, and days and months later
know you have not breathed the same way since

Horizons

to the sparrows in the terminal at Mitchell Field, Milwaukee

all your life you have to travel somewhere
crumb to crumb
floor to soffit, bubbler to piano,
the spread of atrium
and your still point an immense sanctum
that holds the pattern of your flight

and if you knew how wide
    was the offering of your sky,
        how far would you fly?

all your life you have to roost somewhere
plastic tree
girder or spar, baggage claim,
the top of a shop, security,
and your sanctuary whatever peace
can keep safe winged desire

and if you knew how unblessed
    was the safety of your nest
        how long would you rest?

Seven Portraits

thérèse
you also had your cold mornings
fumbling at your cincture with fingers
dull with sleep in the five o'clock dark

you knelt down to pray and at length
tilted face down, asleep

and surely even those moments when
wicked off of strength you turned to sand
yet kept going till you fell

you had no feelings for currency
still your alchemy the best: the trust
that turns all to love

jane
there are some secrets better kept
quite plain, and who would have guessed
all you hid under that hideous cap

now hopelessly illustrious, smothered in
admiration, and all the more unknown

and happily no one saw you when
you penned a world from your heart
your laughing illuminations, your darknesses
alike hidden in the quickened ink

sequestered in that delicious domain
only the unknown writer knows

max
what if there were nothing more real

than that sound from your flute, and
suppose it was more than what it was?

I will show you a mystery: love unsummed
the measure of your life, and all your genius
not what was, for being too small

in a life drawn by lines of music
or questions, heard but not touched
except by the real

you came to the end with only one answer
and the only one that mattered

dorothy
from the beginning the play's the thing
and if this is not drama enough
for a mind so enamored of words

you'll conjure a series of mysteries
for the whimsy, the bills, the joy, until

the characters stroll onto the stage
and you're back where you started

and now you're in deep, in mysteries
so real it takes retelling them to know
till you're left with the last labor

of a mind overmastered by truth

gwen
after years of burning at others' doors
never quite welcome nor whole
you at last found the key in seclusion

and if you could keep the world away
enough to clear your heart between your

soul and vision, the aperture

however small, would clarify, and open
on form and color, shape and light
and faithfully, you knelt

God's little artist, and transcribed
the luminous peace of the house at rest

flannery
because I'm good at it, but also
because you had to, no questions asked
obey

you looked out and saw a sky of violent grace
coming down with glory on an unsuspecting
bamboozling, bamboozled world
your duty to somehow report this weather
nobody seems to be bothering with

you have to take it so seriously
just because it's real
it's the grimace of indifference that's the lie

jackie
you take that catgut, wooden box, and bow
yourself taken to feed that fire inside
to where your blood flows in the bow
to where it sings in the string

you have to submit to be consumed
you have to transmit that inner flame
to where it flies off the bow, off
the page

what's left of you is ashes
and the music goes out to the spheres
and the rest is not our business

Our Lady of the Whippoorwills

They start again around four AM, punctually, just when
I settle for silent prayer. First distant, from the woods.
Then one comes to circle the house: *Get Maurice!*

Garage side, then a few minutes later, on the patio.
Get Maurice! Insistent, unceasing. A rhythm of petitions.
Imperative litany. This is the only prayer it knows.

Soon one appears on the icon of Our Lady. Then a whole row,
lined up attentively before her: squat brown speckled birds,
each with a white chin-strap, penny eyes and whiskers.

She solemnly holds one, and the Child Jesus two more.
The angels about them are whirling whippoorwills,
their celestial *Get Maurice!* flaming across the gold leaf.

I pray. For the next hour, like the patient earth, I have
only to listen, bearing in silence all that alights and disappears,
night, myself, whippoorwills, and the unrepeatable dawn.

From the Desert Elders

Whether the demons you battle are this or that

desires walking without or shadows raging within

anything that puts your nose out of joint

is like the mice that eat your grain

You can still be this and yet faithful

You can carry these stones as long as you want

Sooner or later you'll awaken, realize

you can give everything away

What did you come out to see? Fulfillment?

Instead the horizon offers more horizons

chasms and cliffs you hadn't guessed existed

an endless landscape of discovery

Find one spot, and you will be everywhere

Shut up, and the barren emptiness will teach you

Don't fear you will get bored, or perfect

Your learning lasts while you have breath

This is the real language of your conviction

why you read scripture, why you go to church

why you bother to order your life by faith:

to abstain from judging any but yourself

The commercial at the bank tells me

Time is life's most precious commodity.
They have faster service. Online. So I can spend

less time banking and more time living.
At the gas station a guy on a crutch limps

around the truck in front of me to say Hello,
he didn't know Sisters still wore habits.

I confess yes, some do. He says well he has
a piece of history for me. He was in Chicago

as a boy but moved up here when he was ten.
He was three or four, but he remembers

Our Lady of the Angels, the firetrucks,
ninety-five children and nuns. And safer practices

happened because of that. Something
good came of it. Well, that's all. We part.

And I wonder if I missed the moral,
or if all this time living is going to seed,

or if when I was at the bank
I actually stopped living, just for a little.

Three Epiphanies

Mene mene

It wasn't when I heard about you
—no
                    it was when
a bird fluttered out of the sky
and fell twisting at my feet until
I saw the light go from its eyes

and felt within a mountain move,
telescope, and vanish through
some unknown hole—

then I knew

Tekel

On a street in Assisi
I am stopped by a stranger
by the devil's advocate
by the devil

who wants to know only
if I'm Catholic or Anglican
—either or, nothing more—
to pick a brand

And there on a street in Assisi
I pick a brand, and the devil,
the devil's advocate
the stranger

smirks, and says only
"I thought so"
and disappears

Upharsin

This, he said,
after I had confessed
infelicitations, considered
indiscretions, indulgences,

This—
after I
unloaded, protested, paraded
lapses and relapses, broken
laws, intentions, negligence
or malice

This, he said,
is your penance
and your kingdom undivided:
to surrender all your wrath to Love
and all your life to Praise

how it happens

remembering
unfolds
constantly
whatever
necessarily
prose
wonder
glory
embody
gone off
themselves
homeless

Terminally ill with weeks to live

They are logging in the woods, cutting down
the straightest, tallest, oldest. I brace myself
for the openness, the new glades, litter
of branches. I think of you, so full of plans
twenty-eight years ago. This evening
there are five crows jumping around in the oats.
Everything tells me a story about you.

I once read about a woman who took part
in an experiment of believing she had only
weeks to live. They were told at the start
You are living your life based on a fallacy.

Everything becomes something else. This tree,
books, that one, someone's house, again.

At the end she said *I've stopped worrying, I'm free.*
I'm so ready to do everything I've been putting off.
Then she died. Nobody had expected that.

At twilight the hermit thrushes are still singing
over the wreckage, *o holy, holy,* their song impervious
to every memory, every loss, their love
silent muscle for whatever comes.

Angelus, Art Institute of Chicago

we were visiting old friends/ at the Art Institute
The Solitude of the Soul, White Crucifixion/ A special
Chinese bowl, platinum prints/ *Music in Green & Blue*/ Seeing

where the conversation would go/ this time, what would
they say/ You remember that woman (a visitor, not a painting)
who stopped us in Nineteenth-Century Romanticism

and told me/ *O Sister there is a beautiful Annunciation*
you should go see/ in a voice that said/ she was seeing stars/
angels/ she'd been knocked out of her socks

And I thought, oh yes: here is someone who knows art isn't a matter for
talking at, who knows that listening stipulates reverence, demands total
faith, even surrender, maybe the death of the life you walked in with. She
will go out the glass doors, down the steps to the city, carrying within her
that new astonishment, attuned to the awe of everything. If she wants, she
can transfigure the world.
Amen, amen, amen.

Breakfast reading

for Fred

I read the peony over breakfast
each petal a book of light
a flush of color played in form:
coral   calm   breath-of-pink

each wrinkle and swell an abyss
of subtlety, each curl an invitation
each hue a pulse of intoxicating sound
I want to hear ad infinitum

this bloom a cupped ear that heard
undreamt-of bends of light, an antenna
that offers the secrets of the cosmos
for anyone who wants to hear

I'm reading a vocabulary of light
that is my heart's first language
and I couldn't translate a single word
it renders lovely gibberish: *nuances of woof*

why does nobody else stop to read
here in plain view on the table, this
small horticultural supernova, so intense
I can't tear myself away, can't take it all in?

no thriller could be more gripping
did I spill coffee down my front? slobber
cereal on the table? who cares? today
I've found a new love, a true master

I want to say "Forget Tanner, Rachmaninoff,
forget Riemenschneider. What are they all
beside this one peony? This ephemeron
will feed me for the rest of my life."

variation and fugue on a happy liturgical typo

Lead us into the solemn joy of sanctity and the heavenly peach which passes all understanding.

—*from the Pentecost novena*

o heavenly peach that passes all understanding
o great peach of heavenliness
o peach that tastes of heaven
o heaven beyond all understanding

o understanding that cannot grasp peaches
o understanding that falls so far short of heaven and peaches
o peach so great there is none like on earth
o earth of small unsatisfying peaches

o peach surpassing Infinitely James's Giant Peach
o immeasurable peach

o solemn joy of sanctity and heavenly peach
o heavenly peach of such solemn joy

o peach of surpassing delectableness
o delectableness known only to heaven
o heaven that purveys such marvels of peach

o marvel of beatific peachiness
o beatific peach of heaven
o god grant us your heavenly peach

Fat quarters

Glued a chocolate caramel in the live-trap
caught another mouse this morning. Let it go
behind the barn, with a blessing.

Guy at Copps asked me, "Are you allowed
to wear red with a habit?" and smiled at my scarf.
I said yes. Bought four red poinsettias and some beer.

A Christmas card today told me Frost's
"The Gift Outright" is hope for our nation.
Poetry as essential, as hope.

Thirty gift-wrapped books with bows
in the corner of my room, and a brand new
twenty-inch chainsaw. How do you wrap a chainsaw?

Just after the solstice the sun goes down
a blinding eye, behind the barn.
We let it go, with a blessing.

Antoine de Saint-Exupéry changes his mind

Leon, you asked about that little book
I was writing in America, about the prince.
Well, I decided it was too much trouble.
Who would want to read it? The world
is changing too much. People have lost
all sense of imagination and spirit. There
is no way my book would be understood,
even by children; better not to bother
at all. So I threw it on the fire, see? No loss.
Someday, when I see you again, maybe
I'll tell you how the story went.

Antoine de Saint-Exupéry in Moscow, 1935

On the trail of larger quarry Saint-Exupéry
unearths a cache of forgotten French governesses
left over from an almost erased era. Their protégées
are since exiled or executed or soon to be. Wizened
relics, lost to history, they weep to be found, flaunt
his presence to the neighbors, loudly clank liqueur
glasses. Drunk with acknowledgement,
they proudly show off a Russian friend
who can pronounce his chief triumph
in French they taught him: *In 1906*
I played roulette at Monaco.

A day in advance of his official invitation
Saint-Exupéry is invited onto the Maxim Gorky
by an excited official who cannot wait until
the following day. He is the first foreigner ever
to be invited onto the flying propaganda office.
The following day while Saint-Exupéry is elsewhere,
the Maxim Gorky explodes over Moscow
while executing an aerial display of Soviet prowess
gone terribly wrong.

Riding eastward to the Russian border
into the dark across a troubled continent,
Saint-Exupéry has a sudden vision,
confronted with carloads of sleeping
Polish émigrés being returned from France,
of a golden-haired and prodigious future
assassinated in its first youth.

Gottfried Wilhelm Leibniz in three instances

I enter a library, 1654
    and know I have found my love, my destiny.
    I can smell it, sandwiched in these papers—
    a way to see the order of everything. I, too,
    will make a library, a compendium
    of knowledge for the glory of God
    and the public good. I grow fat on books.
    From now on, I will direct everything to the same aim,
    in all things, even little verses at school, lacing
    my boots, scrubbing my face in the morning

I sit for my portrait, 1703
    and admit again to Herr Scheits how it's hard
    to sit and not work when there is so much to do.
    He nods, smiles, lights up when I begin to discuss art.
    Are not these too useful works and beautiful discoveries?
    It is an image of how One made all things out of nothing.
    He is delighted to have an audience to enlarge his thoughts.
    I watch him watching me, salved with appreciation, happily
    mixing his pigments, the brush taking his dictation. Afterwards
    I congratulate him on my nose, the lively look of my eyes.
    He seems pleased he has caught my likeness, my character.
    We agree his work will please, very much, Madam the Electress

I am confined to bed, November 1716
    and think of her, and others who surpassed me.
    We have done our best with history, and it will never
    be finished, only progress. If next week I do not rise
    to greet the day, still I have done what I could;
    it is for the industry of others to retrieve the rest
    from the darkness. This, too, is of a piece with everything,
    this hiatus from work, this abysmal pain. The universe
    is here, too, unsurpassably good, and I will go on
    learning without end. Even if to some, *non liquet*—

I will find a way to show those who understand
with my life if nothing else—
Inclinata resurget

Archduke

for Max

"Let's do the *Archduke*," they said, like children about to enjoy a treat ...
—Edward Greenfield, recounting the Barenboim Trio

Supposedly, you are like the rest
of us, but for you we have a double standard, choices
    nobody else can choose.

You even come with a different
language, flights, dreams and idioms not suited to our usage,
    and cannot make yourself heard

Except by virtue of what will set
you apart, and everything we use even feels different for you,
    fits you like a poorly cut suit.

You have to fall back on using
other peoples' paradigms, things you weren't meant for.
    We weigh you down with them.

And if I say *things you weren't meant*
for, I mean you simply have no idea what we mean by limits,
    nor do you understand fear.

In a world where measure
is the highest authority, you came with one we do not know,
    beyond all known boundaries.

You are one of God's mistakes,
one who snapped the mold, unable to comprehend
     any measure less than your reach.

Some cosmic joke was played
on you: switched at birth, you belong to a planet, a universe,
     where no one would find you singular,

Where you could live as if
you were other than all that we use to define you, as if
     you were not your distinction.

Outside our definitions, you are
immune to established orders of limitation, perception,
     all our terms of navigation.

You have some compass unknown
to us, your true north a point off all our charts,
     a star only you can see.

I have heard you abandon yourself
to that impulse we call unthinking mastery, possessed
     by an elevation that rescinds distance.

What carries you away draws us
after you, as if you were right to be unbounded, as if
     you made us more ourselves.

in the place where you gathered you were scattered

to the memory of the father of a poet

This doesn't happen to us all—only,
(mostly) to those of us who net and glean
(patiently) from forms: word or shape or sound,
and form again by ear or eye or hand
only to be broadcast in a thousand
parts, gift to find anew through means first found;
or those obliged by force of temperament (or fate)
all sense to coinhere, and reap and sow
in kinesis at a single blow. No,

for you it was a bit different, you see,
you fished only most literally. Still,
this too sustains, and reckons as much skill
and soul, and likewise gives abundantly
alone to those who stand, and search, and wait.

You teach me light (for a Ner Tamid)

after Jeanie Tomasko

Day, don't say *day*, say prismatic ocean
invisible snow, passe-partout

Not *sun*, say luminous fruit,
roving oracle, impossible monocle—

no, not luminous, say sacred attire
say you are rayed with benediction

that runs merrily to the fringes of your sight—
Don't say *sight*, say the span of your soul

say your miraculous being exposed
like a flame, dance that knows no shadows

say no shadows will ever comprehend it
no floods can sweep it away

Say your heart is an unquenchable lamp—
no, not *flame, lamp,* say immensity, peace

in a point, tree of shimmering blessing,
stupendous unpronounceable bush

Cranes, Easter morning

Thought that first imagined sound
then heard: thin fiddleheads of song
furled up from the woods' Lenten array
speckling the bright air white

Look: even the ear can see how light
can verse and has a master's way
with form. What is not found
within its art is fear

Look: it ribbons the wind, long
and shaped like notes in flight,
and finding field, and skies
fit for sowing the word, disappear

trailing their alleluias: *Don't stop here*
                    Arise

The girl who could swim in the sea

"Miracle-child has whole ocean as her playground"

So how long have you been swimming like this?
Oh, I don't know, a long time!

And you can swim anywhere at all?
Not anywhere, but almost anywhere. Some places you shouldn't go, or you can't.

Like where?
Very very deep places. I can't go there, it's too heavy. Or some places where the water is bad or there's garbage, or with currents that are *really strong*. Places like that. And I don't go where it gets really cold!

How did you begin to swim all over the ocean?
I don't know. I just started swimming.

Was there someone who taught you?
Someone told me I could do this, and that I was the only one. I had to rescue someone, and it was scary because there was a storm, but I went.

Who told you this?
Someone very close to me.

Your parents?
No.

What is it like to swim anywhere at all?
I don't know, you just go! I like it a lot, it's really fun. Sometimes I go very fast and sometimes I like to go slow, and sometimes I just take a current.

With the ocean so vast, how do you navigate? Do you ever have difficulty knowing where you're going?

You kind of feel your way. You just know after a while. I don't have any problem. Sometimes I don't know, but it's OK.

Do you ever get lost?
Sometimes.

Is that scary?
No.

Do you get lonely, swimming by yourself?
No, I like to swim by myself. Besides, there's the sea.

Is there ever any danger from sharks?
No. They aren't interested in me.

What's the longest you've ever spent underwater?
I don't know. I don't notice.

You haven't taken a watch?
Someone once gave me a watch you could use underwater, but I forgot to look at it. It felt too heavy so I took it off. I think a fish ate it!

How do you breathe underwater?
I don't know, I'm just OK. I go and I'm OK. It's normal, it's like breathing.

Do you ever get the bends?
No.

What's the most interesting thing you've ever seen in the ocean?
Oh gosh, so many things.

Can you pick one?
Hmmm . . . Can I think about it for a while?

You mentioned you don't go very deep. Doesn't it get very cold if you go even a little deep?
It depends. Some places are always cold and some aren't ever. And there are currents. Besides, if you are there a lot, it doesn't feel the same.

What is your favorite place?
I don't know, I like so many places a lot!

Is there any place you like in particular, for any reason?
Well, yeah. I like to go to a middle depth where I can still see the sunlight a little, but there's almost no current and it's very still and quiet. Sometimes I just kinda sit there a while and listen.

What do you hear?
Sounds from far away, boats, fish, rumblings in the earth, things like that. But sometimes, if you're in the right spot, and you're quiet, you can hear the light.

What does light sound like?
I don't know, like nothing really, you just hear it.

Do you have any advice for anyone who would want to swim all over the ocean?
No.

Nothing at all, from all your experience?
No, they'll figure it out.

Life-size Fiberglass Galápagos Tortoise

February in a big-box store, I was stopped
in my tracks between the lawn doo-dads and
the hoses. Someone had left in the aisle, as
though it had nowhere to go, a Galápagos

Tortoise, frozen in mid-stride, pointing its
beak at me. Nonplussed, I left. But ever since,
I'm haunted by possible uses for a Tortoise.
It could have an office you could never give
to a real tortoise, and be a slow, meditative

seat. It could offer a mini-Galápagos immersion
experience in your own yard. Save paradise,
stay home. It could remind you that Darwin
sailed on the *Beagle*, then that Paul of Tarsus
sailed on the *Castor & Pollux*, one of the ships
that did not shipwreck with him. From this

you would think of the role of turtles in creation.
Paul and Charles would stroll round the garden,
carefully sidestep the tortoise, discussing
that stack of turtles, Charles's amazing
spectacles, and what it would be like

to be a child again,
seeing a world you had never imagined,
and knowing the place for the first time.

The Secret Lives of Poets

for a nurse and an entomologist

"We may feel bitterly how little our poems can do … yet it has always been true that poetry can break isolation, show us to ourselves when we are outlawed or made invisible, remind us of beauty where no beauty seems possible, remind us of kinship where all is represented as separation."
   —Adrienne Rich

Sandburg was a Socialist, Powers was a nun
Eliot a banker, which doesn't seem like fun

Neruda was a diplomat, (Neruda was a pseudonym)
RS Thomas, clergy, what measure suited him

Wordsworth was a taxman, Dickinson, a recluse
Stevens was a lawyer (it must have been some use)

Spenser was a secretary, Kenyon was a translator
Silverstein a veteran, Yeats a Senator

Clampitt was an editor, Rich an activist and teacher,
(but Byron, Lord, he was just rich) and Donne the king's preacher

Lorde was a librarian, Bradstreet was a homemaker
Shelley was a gadabout, Anon was a Shaker

But none of them could live on poems: a song won't get you hired.
"Confessing" poems won't pay the bills; "profession" is required.

"Writer," yes, and "artist" too, or "starving artist" possibly;
"Musician," "dancer," "critic," "sculptor," "novelist," could charge a fee.

But "poet" doesn't make the cut; of all the arts, it's semaphore,
the provenance of prophets, exiles, rebels, minstrels, metaphor,

no employment but a symptom: some mission, syndrome,
joke, affliction, sibyl you become.

Trees in Europe, 1000 CE

to the Tausandjährigbaum at Egenburgerhof

I have seen little pictures of them, enormous and mythic
or in careful orchards, or small and plaiced, caught
in youthful loveliness in illuminated gardens,

or stately on broad canvases, extras to epic events:
accessory to saints, or to the drama of salvation.
They knew all about that—salvation is casting

their seeds to the wind before they get felled
by something—mistletoe, or storms, or illness, or
a majesty that made them too suspect to men

and their ideas. They waited out their wars.
They are long gone now, and some of their atoms
(some of their stories) have become some of mine,

while some of the stories we share are still growing.
For before anyone had made a *Millennium*, or
a *Schism*, you sprouted, and endured to bear

arms that seemed to circle the sky, with a trunk
like a house, a thousand years under your bark,
a thousand years of seasons, of birds and their nests,

you have seen them all, and let a thousand years
of seeds and leaves dance off your fingers, each year still
as freshly, gaily naive as the green dress of any sapling.

buttonhole tune

the moon round and ripe
is hollering with light
God's besotted singing telegrams to me tonight

that He loved me I knew
but I blush and eschew
to divulge the secret scandals in these "I-love-yous"

Jim bach seeing

The whole of life lives in the verb "seeing."
    —*Teilhard de Chardin*

Jim bach said I see the sun with my skin and I see
the sky with your words, and I see the wind
with my hair and my face and the sea
with my ears, the sand with my toes and
the town with my nose,
        but I see the stars with
your touch, the moon and the world, the whole
improbable universe
                with your kiss

Where I tried to explain that my clock exploded

On the corner of the Plattnerstraße, kitty-corner from
the Kiliansdom. If you turned west the Domstraße
stretched ahead, a wide avenue that sloped to meet

the Alte Mainbrücke with its weathered rococo saints.
The bridge itself was much older, repaired to an inch
of its life, had made up for lost time. The statues

were all eight feet high on pedestals, people of different
eras who never imagined they'd see such days. Children
leaned over the mended stone rail, throwing pebbles

in the timeless water. You could just see downriver
the Einheitbrücke, still only a few years old, linking
two banks, two worlds. Beyond that the ferris wheel

and fairway of the Kiliansfest. Music was on the wind.
Beer would be flowing. Everyone was out in the streets,
jammed in cafés. Fifty years ago it took only twenty minutes

to destroy almost everything. Time stopped, bells melted.
People vanished. Each gutted minute became a year
of redeeming what could be. The lost nave of the Dom

rebuilt in Romanesque starkness now forever dazzled
by its golden rococo chancel. The shop had clocks
all around the façade, the time in a dozen places.

I told the clerk in my best German . . . *I tried to fix it.*
She smiled sympathetically. What can't be fixed can't last.
I left with a new clock under the peal of bells.

Possible open letter to the Reverend X, former religious superior, theologian, author

Dear Father X,
Look, if I didn't respect you, would I bother saying this? The thing is,
I found something you wrote less than your best. So help me out here.
Maybe it's like this: you didn't really understand
what you were talking about. It sounded reasonable,
it ticked all the boxes, so you wrote it, they published it.
The book got lots of good reviews anyways; you felt those
two paragraphs were a good case for an integral issue. Or maybe
it's like this: you went on a scapegoating spree. There was no need
to research, or look for human faces, it just *fit*:
this tangential point was the problem.
Or maybe this: you were standing up for truth when you slammed
_____ people, having never met one, or had one for a friend,
since snarky columnists and juvenile rants posted online
are better authority, and better tailored to your argument. Whatever.
Sometime, if you have the time, maybe a cup of coffee is in order.
You and a _____ person could chat at a coffeeshop, split a baklava.
I'll volunteer, but I think this time you could pay.
We'll leave all sticky labels at the door.
I won't ask you about your failures as a superior. You won't ask me
about mine. We'll compare habit rosaries. Finances, the headache.
Modern composers we admire. Your eyes will glisten
as you speak of musician friends. I'll tug on my guimpe, animated,
telling anonymous tales about crazy artists I know.
If you think you can take seeing the world anew, you can even
ask me about _____. I'll be frank.
Your brow will knit, hands folded.
Spoons will clink politely. The waiter will pour more coffee.
You'll ask me questions, shoulders earnest. I'll make a cracking joke,
and we'll laugh so hard everyone turns to look.
Suddenly everything will have to be improvised.
You'll order two apple kurabiye, relax in your chair.
I'll uncross my fingers. Someone will sit at the empty table beside us.

You'll wipe your eyes, giggling, scribbling on your napkin thoughtfully,
maybe something that makes you think,
maybe notes for another book,
maybe the beginning of your salvation.

Calling it

Someone said they were sorry
I had lost you, and I had to wonder

on what corner or on what bus seat
I had inadvertently misplaced you

as though some day I could find you
in the utensil drawer, or behind the dryer

like any old object subject to loss,
or as though you were no longer loved

Someone said I was so very blessed
because of all that went well in my life

and I had to wonder what about those
not so blessed, lopped out of the running

dropped off the edge, over the margin
by divine neglect, as though blessed

were the sum of things preferred,
were something I could lose

aide memoire

I'm here today to do what I've never done
in a coffeeshop before: write a poem. It's
because of you. Go ahead and try to fink out
on account of health today. I bet you can't.
I'm remembering all the times you did—
I only did once (I had died of despair). Today
I'm thinking of the Turkish football game
over my shoulder, unintelligible but fascinating
you were once discreetly distracted by, of the
young man just past you, helplessly in love
with the girl across from him, whose fascination
for his companion, unintelligible but fascinating,
I was discreetly distracted by. We were talking
fascinations. Once, after I had died, you let me go
on and on until I was sick of my own voice, sick
and so still alive. Once, you did your best
to eat the baklava I put before you. We talked
memories, milestones. You said once
"I've been thinking a lot about how
I might not be one of the exceptions."
You said once "It reminds me of my dad
in his last months." I said so many times
(to myself, but not to you) "You don't need
to worry. You'll still be around." To myself.
We always argued over whose turn it was
to pay. I said it was mine. You said it was
yours. I strong-armed you into letting me
pay this next time. You acquiesced. Here
I am, I've bought the coffee and the cake.
You didn't eat your half, as usual, so this time,
I ate it for you; I was rude, I didn't even ask
"Are you going to eat that?" We were never

in a hurry to go, there was always more
to say, more not to say, more
to just let go.

I'm in no hurry to leave now, either. No,
don't want to go, but sometimes, you go,
you're done, it's just what you have to do.

from a manual on forgiveness, with exercises, and diagnostics

you live with bearing your own wrath
wanting the enemy to be destroyed by it
your wrath is the god of your wanting

wanting things to be different
can happen like lightning, or
takes time, sometimes

sometimes all you can do to begin
is want it, want it, want it
even when you think it might kill you

it might kill you, but never to begin
is to guarantee that it will
to want is to begin

to begin and keep going means one day
to arrive; and to keep going, desire
more, tell the truth, deny nothing

deny nothing but the hopelessness
of change; and work on this: define
enemy, define *hope*

hope a notch higher, leave the door
ajar to hope, and try, practice
the thought, *X is not the enemy*

the enemy, instead, hides in your seeing

your seeing tells your want
your want spells the key, the lock, and the door
and whatever has mastered your want

and whatever has mastered your want

Miriam of Magdala addresses the seven departed demons

Shame how I pity you: now my glory
is all you despised: to be a woman

No more to fear I will be cast away
by all, as though too base for a story

Nor ever to fear that to be human
is to be the measure that others say

I fear no hurt: look, I dare everything
I am free: I have no terror to lose

You made me hate myself, unbelieving
You made me think I had no mind to choose

Look, self-doubt, and quail: I am Magdalene
and limitless love brought me fruition

Do your worst, men, laws, and institutions—
you cannot ever silence me again

The Guardian Angel Convention

Once, I was taken to the Guardian Angel Convention.
My angel was in a hurry, throwing things together
and in all the fuss dropped me into his pocket.
And just like that we were gone. I'm not sure where
the convention was. Let's say it took no time to arrive.

I'll try to say it just as it happened.
What happened? Well, there was nothing to *see*.
Like Stuart Little, I was deep in a pocket.
I only heard voices. But imagine millions on *millions*
of guardian angels. It was perhaps a regional gathering.
There was a month of joyous greetings and reunions.
And everyone seemed to know everyone.

And they began with singing. They were a happy lot.
And there were loads of seminars; I caught a few titles:
"Dispensing Grace: Helping Your Human Grow Up"
"Vital Skills: Facilitating Total Human Health Even
When They Don't Want It" "Innovators and Mavericks:
New Directions in Guidance" "How to Survive Caring
for an Artist: One Angle on a Common Story"
"Ministering to Shut-Ins: Resources for Guiding
Humans with Intransigent Oppositional Rigor Mentis."
There were more seminars than I could count,
on more issues than I could have fit in my head.
They were all contributors, all listeners, they
were all courtesy and benevolent keenness. And
laughter, always laughter, whatever the topic;
the laughter of those who have a perspective
so dizzyingly vast, nothing is an obstacle, nothing
is an alarm. I wanted to listen, collect some useful
tips, to soak up some of that angelic point of view,
but try as I might it was all over my head, and
my refuge was warm, and I kept falling asleep.

They had their down time too, but it seemed they
never slept, or needed to take five of anything.
They liked to socialize; they must have had soirees.
Certainly they talked, a *lot*. And they told stories:
and this is the embarrassing part. It was exactly like
a crowd of people chatting affectionately about
their cats. How to keep them in line; how dear they
are; all the trouble they get into; oh, their charm.
"I just give his tail a yank" "When she sleeps she's
got the sweetest little smile" "He'll purr all day long!"
"She's like a big lazy lump I have to lug around"
"The innocent looks he gets!" The endearments
were endless, excruciating in their tenderness.
Nobody mentioned claws, or biting, not even my angel.
Nobody groused or vented anxieties. There was no
talk of wars, or violence, or sin. They were just one
lot of angelic devotion, as if every one had a plum,
their jobs were all sinecure, and their charges
of no more cunning or malice than kittens.

Then it was all over, and the next thing I knew
I heard a laugh, and was plucked from my hideout:
"Oh, so that's where you've been!" and got a kiss
on the top of my head. And, yes, you should have
seen the look on my face, like a cat whose dignity
has been perturbed, who has got to go have a hasty
bath, and knows the laughter in the background,
however loving, is somehow, all the same, at its expense.

memento vita

A few days before your sudden death
you awoke suddenly at night
stared into the dark, and your gaze
felt along the wall to the black
intersection of the crucifix, and there

came to you the sudden thought
something amazing, beautiful,
is going to happen, something wonderful
and felt a strange and sudden flash of fear
as if of light

and turned and thought of plans
and business, errands, hopes
and groceries, and at last
fell back asleep

And fear shall be no more

for Marianne Rein

I asked you
where
does the white of the snow
    go after it is gone?

then you said
look,
I want to show you this
    light
    take my hands
    let go

Notes

The Jewish Bride

This is based on a story recounted by Dr Ruth Valerio of her great-great aunt and -uncle, during World War II in Berlin, which is used with permission. The time the woman spent hiding in the allotment shed was seven years.

Seven Portraits

of Thérèse Martin (St Thérèse of Lisieux), Jane Austen, Max Thompson, Dorothy L Sayers, Gwen John, Flannery O'Connor, and Jacqueline du Pré

Jim bach seeing

The word *bach* is a Welsh masculine diminutive and endearment.

Trees in Europe

The farm at Egenburg in lower Franconia was once a medieval grange. Though nearly all of the original buildings are gone a tree that spouted before the grange was ever established is still growing. It is just under 1,000 years old.

Where I tried to explain that my clock exploded

Told from the perspective of 1995. The city of Würzburg was destroyed by Allied bombing in March 1945.

www.ingramcontent.com/pod-product-compliance
Lightning Source LLC
LaVergne TN
LVHW051707080426
835511LV00017B/2782